ENERGY LITERACY

How to Perce'
of Your Spi

Shephe

Summerjoy Press
Laguna Niguel, California
2020

ENERGY LITERACY
How to Perceive and Take Charge of Your Spiritual Well-Being

Summerjoy Press
99 Pearl
Laguna Niguel CA 92677-4818

shoodwin@gmail.com
https://shepherdhoodwin.com

Copyright © 2020 by Shepherd Hoodwin

All rights reserved. No part of this publication may be reproduced, stored in a retrieval system, or transmitted, in any form or by any means, electronic, mechanical, photocopying, recording, or otherwise, without the prior written permission of the publisher, except by a reviewer, who may quote brief passages in a review.

ISBN: 9781654297305

Photograph of Shepherd Hoodwin by John Kilis.

Dedicated to

JOHN FRIEDLANDER

Who teaches me so much

Table of Contents

ENERGETIC HEALTH—An Overview	1
GENERAL CLEARING	10
1 PSYCHIC DEBRIS	15
2 EMOTIONS	17
3 PICTURES AND BLOCKS	20
4 CHAKRAS	22
5 CONTRACTS AND VOWS	23
6 CORDING	25
CLEARING CORDS	26
7 OTHER PEOPLE'S ENERGIES	28
8 ENTITIES AND IMPLANTS	31
CLEARING ENTITIES	33
9 PSYCHIC ATTACK	35
10 EARTHBOUND SOULS	38
11 SOUL RETRIEVAL	40
CONCLUSION	41
RESOURCES	42
ABOUT THE AUTHOR	43
OTHER BOOKS BY SHEPHERD HOODWIN	45

ENERGETIC HEALTH—An Overview

There has been a good deal of increased intellectual understanding among spiritual students during recent decades. I believe that the next frontier is what I call "energy literacy," learning to discern and work with our energy field (aura) in ways that bring healing and greater well-being.

I'm not an expert on it, and this book is by no means comprehensive, but I will share some of what I've learned from channeling Michael, who does powerful energy work through me, as well as from a number of gifted healers and teachers I've worked with. I include three exercises, which are indented, along with practical pointers interspersed throughout the text.

This book is divided into several sections that define different kinds of energetic interference. However, there is overlap among them, and what is true of one may also be for others. If you don't know what you're dealing with, you can ask Spirit to help you with it. Like all skills, "hearing" Spirit (guides, higher self, etc.) and "seeing" energy become easier with practice. Even if you don't consciously perceive, trust that if you ask, you will receive help.

Over our numerous lifetimes, we've developed many deeply entrenched unconscious habits that may be dysfunctional, or at least not ideal or skillful. These include how we run our energy. By becoming aware of them, we can start to make changes. For example, it is common to take on negative energies from others in a well-meaning but misguided effort to help them. We don't really help them and end up burdening ourselves unnecessarily. There are better ways to help. We live in a time when we finally have enough knowledge and tools to recognize and change ancient beliefs and patterns that aren't fully beneficial. We have a lot of work to do!

"Negative" doesn't mean "bad." Our lessons on the physical plane rely on the polarity of positive and negative—compare and contrast. But those of us who aspire to grow more through joy and less through pain, as the Michael entity puts it, will want to reduce contracted (negative) energies in our life that diminish our happiness. Fear and anger are the main negative energies. Fear is designed to help us avoid threats, and anger (the other side of the coin), to push them away. They have a place, but when they become frozen in us, they are no longer relevant to our current circumstances and cause harm, giving rise to emotions such as resentment, shame, and greed, upon which false personality (ego) is built. They bring us pain. Positive energies are those that flow freely and accurately embody the universal forces of love, truth, and beauty. They give rise to qualities such as goodwill, generosity, kindness, and peace. They bring us joy.

ENERGETIC HEALTH

I do a variety of energy exercises most days, often while taking walks, driving, and so forth. If I don't feel well, I can count on them to help me feel fifty percent better after maybe a half hour. I draw these especially from the work of Susannah Redelfs and John Friedlander (see Resources in the back matter). Susannah has a number of useful exercises on her Techniques page on her site. John is the co-author of four excellent books on psychic development. I highly recommend that you check them out. I also invent techniques in the moment to meet particular needs. Although technique is important, there is no right or wrong way to approach energy work—there are many different techniques that can get the job done as vehicles for our intentions.

I usually find a lot of foreign stuff in my field, despite using "protection" ☺ and my intention not to take it on. A certain amount of that is perhaps inevitable for those of us who keep our field wide open, a necessity for channels, psychics, empaths, healers, artists, and the like. However, we can learn to keep it to a minimum and let it pass through without sticking.

The ideal is to have our field filled only with our own energies most of the time, especially from our *essence* (soul). When that is the case, we carry presence, spiritual power, and natural authority. However, most of us (especially women) have been taught not to fill the space around us to the full capacity of our field, to be smaller and not take up much room, so it requires conscious awareness and work to retrain ourselves. When we fill our space with essence, it doesn't conflict with others who are likewise filling theirs; it just makes the whole atmosphere richer.

We have the right to fill the space around us—it belongs to us. When we don't, there's a void that can allow other energies in ("nature abhors a vacuum"). Signs of that include feeling that something is off and being drained. Foreign energies range from the smallest and simplest, such as psychic debris and the energetic equivalents of parasites and insects, to the largest and most complex/intelligent, such as possession by earthbound souls. The middle includes cording, implants, and psychic attack. The principles of releasing them are similar for all. With some skill, it is not difficult to get rid of them if we are aware that they're there. There is no need to fear them, and fear makes them harder to clear. It's similar to brushing our teeth to remove plaque. I jokingly refer to this as "aural hygiene." It's not something we can do once and be done with; it needs to be part of our routine.

It is essential to know that we each are the most powerful one in our own domain. Those with what the Michael teachings refer to as the obstacle of martyrdom believe that their environment is more powerful than they are, and they have an investment in being a victim because they believe that it helps them gain worth. It can be harder for them to use their power to take control of their field. Their first priority is to "photograph" their obstacle and recognize that it is a false belief, that they have worth just for existing.

The roots of unhealthy energetic connections can go back to childhood. Children are generous in their willingness to try to help or carry others, especially their parents or other caregivers. They see it as being in their self-interest, because if their parents die, they might die, too. (We see that with animal companions as well, who sometimes take on some of their person's illness or unhappiness.) In psychological terms, these are boundary issues. Setting good boundaries applies to the realm of energy as well as to the outer world.

Sometimes we are reluctant to release negative energies we carry from others even when we know they are harming us. It's a good idea to explore what our conscious or unconscious payoff is in keeping things the way they are. Maybe we feel unloved and see carrying them as a way to be needed. Perhaps we feel responsible for some bad thing that happened in the past and are trying to pay penance. Or maybe we just want to help, and don't know better ways to do that.

Buddhism teaches the merits of emptiness or "nothingness." When we empty ourselves of foreign energies, we might feel lonely or strange at first—we're not used to it—and may avoid releasing our "stuff" for that reason. But when we fill ourselves from within, we learn new ways of being that are ultimately much more comfortable. It is often the case with positive change that we need to be willing to go through an uncomfortable transition stage to get there.

Although a certain amount of energetic pollution is a hazard of the physical plane for everyone, we can also attract it due to unresolved issues. For example, our stored anger and fear can attract entities that feed off of it (like attracts like) and incite more anger and fear because they want to keep themselves fed. Trauma can rip open our field, and if it isn't healed, it can continue to leave us vulnerable despite remedial work. In such cases, correcting the core issue is the only solution.

Since the feminine is receptive, women are more prone to taking on external negative energies, as well as men with high female energy. In addition, those who are sensitive, nurturing, ill, injured, and especially, substance abusers, are more vulnerable.

With all psychic work, it's important to be humble and not be too certain about what we're picking up. I would never, for example, say to another person that he was psychically attacking me. I could be wrong, and if I'm correct, it's probably not being done consciously, so talking about it won't achieve anything. When we have confidence in our skills, we simply handle it on our end and are done with it. We live in an imperfect, messy world with a lot of negativity. If we are on a conscious spiritual path, we choose to meet it with love, which is the only real antidote to it.

You can use the techniques here for clearing negative energies both in yourself and others. When working with others who have asked for your help or given you permission, you can coach them to do the work themselves while you observe and support them. Many people are surprised to find how much they're able to see and do. However, if they aren't able to tune in, you can do the work for or with them. If you're working with someone who is not in a position to cooperate consciously, seek permission from their essence. It is not appropriate to enter another person's field without it.

So often, we receive requests on social media and elsewhere to send healing energy to those dealing with health challenges. John says that, in many cases, this results in their energy field being crowded, and as a result, they contract. He suggests that instead of going into their field, we observe their energy and notice what lights up in our own field in reaction to what isn't moving freely in theirs.

If we then explode our "matching pictures" (covered below), we can offer assistance to them without interfering when we may not have permission.

This book is built on the idea that work in consciousness is real, that what we do in ourselves can communicate through the ether to others. For example, we can communicate with other people's essence mentally, or offer energetic healing that gets results. Those who have not experienced this are likely to be skeptical, but if they are open, they can test it for themselves. Although prayer is frequently misunderstood as asking God for something that S/He would not otherwise give, when it succeeds in helping others, it uses the same principles that allow the exercises here to work.

Energy fields are complex and multi-layered, and people have different ways of perceiving, so we won't all "pick up" the same things. It's possible for several analyses of a field to be correct at the same time, each contributing different parts of the puzzle.

Energies may show up as colors, shapes, or textures. If you are not visual, perceive them in your own way: sensing, feeling, knowing, hearing, and so forth. If you're not getting anything, imagine them; pretty soon, real perception will come.

Those who are gifted healers tend to have a high and substantial vibration. A higher vibration is simply one that is faster and finer than a lower one, and can influence it to vibrate more quickly and finely. A faster vibration can shake out stuck energies, and a finer one can correct distortions, resulting in healing and greater harmony. Energies from nonphysical planes are, by definition, higher in vibration. That is why those who channel them can bring healing.

Energy work is an excellent tool but is not a substitute for taking care of our health in other ways, such as seeking medical care (both holistic and mainstream)—it is a supplement. It is usually a good idea to take a multipronged approach to solving any problem. Similarly, it can be helpful with mental and emotional issues, but doesn't necessarily take the place of effective therapies.

Whenever we're doing healing work of any kind, we can call upon to assist whatever higher beings we feel connected with. That could include religious archetypes such as angels, saints, Jesus, Mary, Buddha, Quan Yin, Krishna, etc. I like to call on Mother and Father God, which to me represent the purest versions of the divine feminine and masculine; I can feel their energies palpably. The universe is full of consciousnesses that embody certain qualities. For example, we can state, "I call upon divine (or 'pure,' if you don't like words with religious connotations) love to help heal this and fill me with its energy. Thank you." Offering thanks to your helpers is an important part of the process, completing the circle. Other consciousnesses include peace, joy, freedom, goodness, aliveness, wisdom, purpose, and so forth.

Holding simultaneously a recognition of what is (the lower) and our vision (the higher) generates creative tension that brings evolution. For example, seeing blocked energy while holding a vision of freedom and clarity can help the block release.

This book focuses on foreign energies, but of course we can generate plenty of negative energies from within, too. When they spring from deeply held beliefs, they will keep returning until we change the beliefs. We can't do that until we become aware of what our beliefs are. That requires self-observation. Holding the intention to allow our thoughts, feelings, and energies to be in accord with truth, love, and beauty, to the best of our ability, moves us increasingly into positivity.

Here is an all-purpose meditation for working with your field:

GENERAL CLEARING

> Tune in to your energy field. Perceive (visualize, hear, sense, know, or whatever works for you) and feel it. Ask your essence to help you fill this sphere with your essence energy. Check your

field for soundness. Use your imagination to fill any holes or breaks. Stay with it until it is sound.

Ask that it resonate only with the pure universal frequencies of love, truth, and beauty. Feel this happening.

Ask the earth to ground you in whatever way is in the highest good. Tune in to the center of the earth and feel the flow of energy from it into your body, and the flow of your body's energy into the earth. Feel how your body is comforted by earth energy.

Ask that all debris energies in your field be released and flow into the center of the earth for purification and recycling.

Ask your inner self to "light up" (reveal) all energies that don't belong to you, and send them back to their owners. Include those of both living people and those who are on "the other side." Scan for family members, friends, coworkers, former schoolmates, and so on. You can ask, "Who does this belong to?" but you can also send back energies even if you don't consciously know who the owner is. (Energies without an owner are debris and can be sent into the earth or sun.) Imagine a strong force emanating from your heart sending them back to wherever they belong. You cannot "fix" energies imprinted by other people—only their owners can do that. It's like a lock to which you don't have the key. However, it is supportive to send them back with love and the confidence that the owner can productively handle them.

Invite parts of yourself that have been trying to get your attention to have the spotlight for as long as they need it. Let unresolved anger and fear expand, becoming as big as they need to in order to move freely. Observe them unwinding until they are at rest as pure energy without charge. Listen to whatever inner voices need to express. Thank them.

Once again ask that only those energies that resonate with the pure frequencies of love, truth, and beauty remain in your space.

Open your crown and ask to be washed with light from above. Feel a flow moving down through your body into the earth. After this is established, at the same time notice a flow moving from the earth up through your body and out the top of your head heavenward. Notice how natural it feels to connect heaven and earth.

Ask your essence and guides to create protection all around you, on all levels of being, from uninvited, intrusive energies and beings.

ENERGETIC HEALTH

Affirm that your energy field belongs only to you, and that you have the perfect right to claim and purify it.

IF YOU WISH TO COMMUNICATE WITH SPIRIT, CONTINUE ON:

Ask your essence to connect you with your primary spirit guide (or whatever guide or teacher is most appropriate in the moment), and only that one being. Ask your essence to nod your head yes when that connection is in place and strong.

(If nodding doesn't work for you, use whatever does. Some people, for example, lean forward for a yes and back for a no; some notice a sensation such as a change in temperature. You can also use a pendulum, or simply ask to hear a yes or no in your thoughts. It might take some practice to start recognizing signals from your essence and guides.)

Ask questions and write down or record the answers. If any answers don't seem right, ask specific questions for clarification. Go slowly and carefully.

What comes from Spirit is more subtle than what comes from ego and is relatively free of bias. If in doubt, at any point you can ask your essence to nod your head yes or no to questions such as, "Am I making a clean connection?" or "Is this my primary spirit guide?" If you get a no to the latter, ask questions to determine who it is, such as "Is this my mind?" or "Is this a subpersonality needing attention?" If you get a yes, go back to giving your subconscious a chance to have your undivided attention until you reach peaceful neutrality. Then return to asking to connect with your guides.

When you're complete, thank your guide(s) and ask that it, your essence, and all beloved higher beings continue to fill your field with the protection and richness of love, truth, and beauty.

1 PSYCHIC DEBRIS

The world is full of all kinds of psychic flotsam that can become caught in our field. It's like allergens that we may not see but affect us nonetheless. This debris is in the "air" and can settle like dust in our aura, causing us to feel unclear. This can be an especially big problem for artisans (one of the seven roles—soul types—defined by the Michael teachings), whose auras tend to be large and diffuse. I often recommend to them that they imagine a rainstorm of light washing their aura a couple times a day; it's not a bad idea for the other roles, too. The purpose is to instruct and make space for our inner self to cleanse itself, and when we pay attention to a process, we empower it.

Thought forms are mental debris. Unlike entities (discussed below), they have no will; they are like recorded messages. When they are stuck in our field, they can get in the way and be disruptive. They can come from individuals or organizations such as the Church. For example, a loved one in a lot of pain might have formed a repeating thought form, "I want to die." If we picked it up, it may play like a tape loop in our head, too, long after our loved one was no longer suffering. John teaches to clear thought forms by duplicating them and superimposing the duplicate on the original, making it implode. It's worthwhile to explore why we attracted a particular thought form. In the example above, current frustration or fatigue might attract a death wish thought form.

2 EMOTIONS

It's amazing how often emotions (as well as thoughts and energies) that we assume to be ours are not. Those of us who are sensitive and open can be highly connected to those around us. I remember once feeling wretched out of the blue. After a while, I thought of my grandmother, tried to call her, and discovered that she was in the hospital and had been calling out my name. It's useful to ask, "Is this mine?" If we get a yes, we can ask "What percent?" This can help us release what isn't ours but we had been identifying with and therefore holding onto. Consider them messages that have now been delivered; they no longer need to "ping." We can act on them as appropriate.

There are also pieces of denied emotions from people we don't know, both living and dead, floating around that can get stuck in our energy field. Sometimes these have appeared to me like characters in old movies, stereotypical and without subtlety, revealing just one emotional quality. For example, one looked a bit like a bitter W.C. Fields character; another, like a victimized Nellie tied to the railroad tracks. Their flatness is a clue that they're debris and no longer connected to a living intelligence, since real emotions are complex. We can use our imagination to dissolve them into light, breaking them down like compost.

We deny or push away emotions when we consider them to be unacceptable. Although some emotions can be destructive when acted out inappropriately, all our emotions contain our energy and need to be evolved and integrated if we are to be whole. Rather than regarding some emotions as being bad, it's more useful to think of them as giving us information we can use for growth.

There are many techniques for releasing stuck emotions that originate in us. The simplest is to be with them meditatively, in love and compassion, letting their energy expand, evolve, and integrate into our psyche. This dissipates the electric charge characteristic of stuck emotions, bringing calm. In fact, all forms of meditation can help us improve our energy when we are being with what comes up and/or raising our vibration. I also frequently use the Emotional Freedom Technique (EFT—see Resources), also known as "tapping," to clear patterning using acupressure points.

Another technique is to ask our body what emotions it wants to release, and let it move and make sounds as it wants to. The results can be strange, but this can bring relief. Decades ago, I worked with a gestalt therapist. I regularly pounded pillows and the like in order to release old stored anger. It usually climaxed in tears. A value of such dramatic emotional release practices is that they make it clear that we're carrying around a lot of unresolved emotions in our subconscious. Before that, I had been convinced that I was never angry. However, such techniques make for a lot of wear and tear. When we can release effectively in gentler ways, it's worth doing so.

3 PICTURES AND BLOCKS

Pictures are frozen memories from past experiences, often traumatic, that need to be released so that healing can occur. They are made up of thoughts, emotions, and energies. We all have them. When we're triggered by other people or situations, it's because they're bringing to the surface "matching" pictures that the outer event reminds us of. Becoming aware of them gives us an opportunity to deal with them. "Exploding" matching pictures, as taught by the Berkeley Psychic Institute, is an efficient way to release them. We can simply ask our inner self to light up matching pictures. Then we can "put them in a rose" in front of us and explode it. The fewer pictures we have, the less we magnetize negativity.

We are traumatized when we have an experience we are not equipped to handle—our "circuits" become overloaded. We freeze because we don't know what to do—we can't make sense of what happened. Part of us becomes stuck in that moment. Healing requires engaging with that frozen part of self and showing it that the trauma is no longer occurring, fast-forwarding it to current time so that it can begin to unwind. Maybe we can now make sense of what happened from our current perspective. This process is part of how we evolve. As we successfully handle past traumas, we are less likely to become traumatized in the future—we grow stronger.

Blocks are stuck energies that may or may not have pictures. An example might be a fear lodged in our heart that we experience as a knot of tension. As with pictures, we can ask essence to light up blocks, put them in a rose, and explode it. Repeat as necessary. I also like to imagine exploding stuck energies using the sun's power.

We have many layers of "stuff" that are impossible to release all at once. We "unpeel the onion" a layer at a time. If we deal with what's coming up now, the next layer will present itself. Releasing pictures and blocks is a long-term process.

Techniques like these can save a lot of therapy. On the other hand, fully releasing might require more in-depth therapeutic processes. However, exploding pictures and blocks, and the other techniques outlined here, can't hurt and are likely to speed up healing.

4 CHAKRAS

There is much written about the chakra system. We can all benefit from being more aware of it. Keeping chakras too open or large is as bad as keeping them too closed or small. They need to be flexible and responsive to our needs, and be kept clean and unblocked.

Virtually every person gets tangled up in other people's stuff, which is partly why the world is such a mess. Most people don't know that there are other ways relationships can be handled: they think it's either that or putting up a wall. John teaches not to try to connect with others through our second (emotional) chakra, but instead to use our fifth and sixth chakras to communicate, which allows for intimacy without entanglement. Insisting that others change or agree with us keeps us entangled with them, resulting in a loss of our spiritual power. Accepting "what is" and letting others make the choices that are theirs to make, while we exercise the full range of our own choices, is a key to spiritual growth.

5 CONTRACTS AND VOWS

There's a saying that "You create your own reality" (YCYOR), which originated from Seth channeled by Jane Roberts. We don't create *everything* that occurs in our life, because other people are also creating their reality, and it overlaps with ours. But we are the dominant creator of our own reality, and we attract things based on our vibration and beliefs.

If something unfortunate happens once or twice, we might be able to write it off as what Michael calls a "hazard of the physical plane." But we should pay close attention to repeating patterns, as they almost always suggest ingrained beliefs or other stuck energy.

Negative soul contracts and vows are examples. Let's say that in a past life, your family was murdered when you spoke out against a repressive regime, and you vowed to keep your mouth shut so that would never happen again. You placed a block in your fifth (throat) chakra that remains to this day, preventing you from expressing yourself freely. Understanding why you made that vow and withdrawing it can help get the energy moving again. Past-life therapy can be helpful in such a situation. You might replace it with a vow to express yourself wisely, with sensitivity to what is likely to be helpful. Stating aloud with conviction, "I withdraw (the old vow)," and "I vow (the new one)," might be enough to get the job done

Or maybe you made a contract on a soul level to help others no matter what the cost was to you. At the time, that was your highest vision, but it no longer is. (The soul may be more aware than the personality, but it doesn't always make smart decisions; after all, it is incarnate to evolve.) You can change that contract to help others in a win/win manner as much as you can. Again, you might want to speak aloud and/or write down that you are amending this contract.

Perhaps as a child, your parents fought a lot, and you vowed that you would never have a relationship like that, but your immature mind defined that too broadly to exclude even disagreements. As a result, you are now blocking all intimate relationships. You can revise that, perhaps instead vowing that you will have love-based relationships with people who have good communication skills, but allowing for imperfections.

Identifying and changing contracts and vows, and our beliefs in general, require a deep dive into the subconscious that might benefit from help from a skilled professional.

6 CORDING

Cords are psychic "suckers" that people attach to others in order to take life force. Cords are not the same as connections (for example, between hearts or minds), which are wider, softer, higher-vibration bands of light that bond and allow sharing but do not pull or deplete.

The mechanism of cording exists so that young children can get supplemental energy from their parents. Since their bodies are small, this is not a significant drain. (We might also allow some cording from invalids for whom we've taken responsibility.) Older children and adolescents may need to cord their parents occasionally, but that should happen less and less as they mature. Ideally, adults attach only to their own inner source. However, many never grow up, and adults who cord others can be a significant drain. They tend to see themselves as not being very powerful, and they cord those they see as being strong. If you are viewed as the strong one in your family, even your parents might be cording you. Some people are loaded with cords, especially caregivers, including therapists, healers, channels, personal trainers, and so on. There are those who both cord others and are corded by others, which creates a particularly tangled mess. We can all benefit from cultivating the knowledge that we are strong and can connect to universal power internally.

CLEARING CORDS

Ask to perceive, in whatever ways you do, all your cords. (Visually, they look literally like cords, thick or thin, in different colors and textures, attached to different parts of our body.) Capture them in white light. Command that they dissolve. You might find that there's additional power in saying, "In the name of the Tao" (or love, essence, the Source, God, etc.), I command …." Scan them all the way to their roots on both ends, continuing to "stare them down" until they dissolve into light. You might notice claw-like prongs on your end anchoring them into your field that you need to unhook. You can address all the cords at once, and then handle the stubborn ones that still remain one at a time.

Fill in the holes the roots left in your aura with a healing color, such as pink or blue, or whatever feels good to you.

Create in consciousness a protective light keeping out further cording and other intrusions; a big golden egg-shaped bubble around you is a good image to use. Form and color aren't important, though—they're just ways to focus your intention.

In your mind's eye, go to the people who corded you. Tell them that, as adults, they don't need to take other people's energy—they can connect with their own source and power. Give them pictures of how to do that: from spirit above them through their crown, from the earth below them through their feet, and from their essence through their heart. Let them know that you won't any longer permit them to cord you.

You may need to repeat this process once or twice a day for a couple weeks, because others have the habit of cording you, and you have the habit of letting them.

Also clear any cords you are attaching to others. Forgive yourself and apologize in spirit to those you corded.

7 OTHER PEOPLE'S ENERGIES

A common problem is taking on pieces of other people's heavy energies, often with the intention of helping them. Priest souls are especially prone to this, seeing themselves as strong and responsible for others. They may intend to clear the energies but lack the skill, or never get around to it. Some people take them on out of curiosity, which is a scholar specialty: "Oh, look at this weird, gnarly piece of energy. Fascinating! I'll keep it for my collection to study later." Scholars can be packrats, and as with their other collections, the gnarly energy can pile up.

Taking on other people's burdens isn't doing them any favors. It is not the same as healing them, whether we're talking about energy or anything else. At best, there can be some short-term relief for them, but if the underlying causes aren't addressed, they will just recreate the negative energies, and we're stuck carrying burdens that aren't our own. Some people I work with are severely encumbered in this way, and the energy work of a Michael channeling session or intuitive reading may focus on the "heavy lifting" of beginning to clear them; sometimes it's like blasting through rock. They may have been accumulating them for many lifetimes. Of course, most people do this unconsciously—they don't know that they're doing it. That's why energy literacy is so important: if we start observing what

OTHER PEOPLE'S ENERGIES

we've been doing all along, we can begin to adopt more helpful practices.

If we take on negative energies that spring from someone else's rigid beliefs, the beliefs are inherent in the energies. Since they are not our beliefs, we can't change them, so trying to help in this way is especially futile. All we can do is return them to their owners. Energies not branded by an owner's energy signature can be destroyed and recycled.

Skilled healers know how to help their clients release negative energies without taking them on, although they probably still need to be diligent about it and do maintenance on their own fields. They might be able to help clients release energies that spring from stuck beliefs, but the energies will regenerate if the clients don't change them. Bathing them in love-based vibrations with which they might choose to resonate may inspire them to do so. Having a vision of a higher state is necessary in order to move toward it. For that reason, living from a high vibration is the greatest way any of us can serve humanity. The current state of the world reveals that many people do not know what love looks and feels like.

Be careful about the healers you allow to work on you. Make sure that their energy and motivations are clean and love-centered. Surprisingly, that's not the case with all of them. I've heard stories, for example, of some who deliberately sabotage clients' field so that they'll return for more sessions. Skillful healers of integrity generally have abundant work.

In addition to what we deliberately take on from others, others often send away pieces of their energy. They may be targeted at us, but more often they are free-floating and we just happen to pick them up or magnetize them. They may be parts of their nature they judge, deny, or don't want to face.

You can use the "General Clearing" exercise above to send back other people's energies. This may be the most important thing we can do for our energetic health. If owners refuse to take them back, ask your guides to handle them appropriately. Some of us have been accumulating other people's energies for thousands of years. It can take many years of work to establish fully healthy fields, but it is well worth it.

8 ENTITIES AND IMPLANTS

Entities are semi-intelligent energies that have taken up residence in our field and don't particularly want to leave. Some are parasitic, and like physical parasites, they can create cravings not natural to us, manipulate us emotionally, and block clear perceptions. They are waste products of the evolution of consciousness, energies cast off that were never properly integrated or otherwise handled. Entities have various shapes and sizes. As with cords, we can work collectively with them, and then individually in more depth with the stubborn ones.

Sometimes we make agreements with entities that we need to revoke in order to release them. For example, if we were lonely as a child, we may have allowed an entity to attach because it promised, "I'll never let you feel lonely again." Subpersonalities may similarly make agreements of which we are unconscious. From the *Huffington Post*:

> Subpersonalities are personas or pieces of the whole of the overall personality that have a life of their own: beliefs, thoughts, feelings, intentions, and agendas. There's the *rebel* and the *martyr*, the *seducer* and the *saboteur*, the *judge* and the *critic*, and a host of others, each

with its own mythology, all co-existing within a person.

Getting to know our subpersonalities therapeutically can be very valuable. Journeywork (see Resources) is one technique for doing this.

Implants are artificial entities made by intelligent beings to influence or monitor us. I worked with a healer once who found one in my left shoulder blade. Interestingly, I had long felt like there was a stone there that no amount of massage therapy could release. After she removed the implant, the feeling went away. She said that it was placed there when I was abducted by aliens at age three. I have no memory of this, but keep an open mind.

I learned the exercise below from healer Cynthia Cross. When I first did it, I found about a hundred entities, and it took me three days of hard work to eliminate them, one at a time. Afterward, I found channeling to be easier; it eliminated a draining, jerky rapid breathing that used to happen when Michael was clearing clients' energy during sessions. The entities were clogging my energy field, and releasing them changed my life. I had worked with several healers on the breathing problem previously, and nothing worked long-term, but this has been a permanent correction.

ENTITIES AND IMPLANTS

Some people might object to making commands, but it's your energy field, and you have the right to determine what is there. Many of these entities are dense and won't respond without a show of strength. Still, you can also be compassionate when working with them; most of them aren't malicious, just lost and misguided.

CLEARING ENTITIES

State the following (speaking aloud can be more powerful):

1. I command that you fully reveal yourself to me. (You should get a detailed picture or feeling.)

2. I command that you stretch yourself to the full reaches of your reality creation. (Making them thin helps dissolve them. See them expand three dimensionally if possible, although some entities just exist in two dimensions.)

3. I command that you be thankful for what you have been. (This is powerful—it removes the charge of judgment and self-judgment, acknowledging that all things play a part in our collective growth and evolution.)

4. I command that you release from all levels and layers of my reality creation *now*. (Then "stare

them down" until they release into the light. Be strong with them.)

Repeat the steps if necessary.

9 PSYCHIC ATTACK

I didn't used to believe in psychic attack, but I've experienced it firsthand. It's part of the dark side of shamanic traditions, such as voodoo, where it can be quite sophisticated. However, it can also result when anyone strongly wishes another person ill, such as in a fit of anger. One might feel it as a jab. Usually it dissipates unless the attacker sustains it, which takes a lot of negative will and imbalance (often found in abusive people).

If you want to avoid psychically attacking others when you're angry, imagine throwing the anger up in the air rather than at the person. To avoid being attacked, try to live transpersonally. That means staying centered, not reacting or taking others' actions personally. Then the attacks have nothing to latch onto and can pass through our field. If we see attackers as enemies, that can perpetuate the cycle. It's always wise to meet negativity of any kind with love, at the same time establishing boundaries.

Becoming aware of what's happening can allow us to take control and expel the intrusions. Such attacks rely on our not knowing what's happening, or if we are aware, on being intimidated. Light is stronger than darkness, love is stronger than hate. I'm reminded of what Glinda said to the Wicked Witch in *The Wizard of Oz:* "You have no power here. Now begone, before somebody drops a house on you, too!"

As with other clearing, it isn't necessary to know who the attacker is; the point is to find the energy in our field and remove it. If an attack is overwhelming, one might want to seek the assistance of a healer—someone joining with us can amplify our power. Furthermore, curses placed deliberately and craftily may be hidden well and take more digging to find (the same can be true of entities). However, once they are, removing them involves the same principles as with other negative energies: lock in on them, command them to leave, and stare them down or explode them until they're gone.

Sometimes, what is perceived as psychic attacks or other energetic intrusions are self-created out of astral substance. Gifted psychics are especially capable of this. Perhaps the perceived attack reflects unresolved inner issues, such as guilt. People might believe that an ex is attacking them as a way of keeping him or her their life, when in fact the ex has moved on. Some may love the drama or suffering, or it may be an expression of the belief that the universe is out to get them. Like so much of what we've discussed here, these things are usually unconscious.

An actual psychic attack may be a karmic repayment. Older souls especially might choose to repay karmas in this way, using lower astral substance, rather than acting them out on the physical plane. (Sometimes souls do this between lifetimes, as well, in the "hell" realms of the lower astral.) We might have prearranged this on a soul level. If it's karmic, we will unlikely be able to do anything about it other than endure it, preferably with grace.

Around 1998, I had several sessions with a healer recommended by another Michael channel whose specialty was removing curses and other forms of psychic attack. It was an education. He also worked on a friend, and her life turned around dramatically. She was part owner of a Caribbean hotel that was being stolen by lawyers. Apparently, they had hired a voodoo practitioner. Within a couple weeks, she got a check for $100,000 she'd been owed and trying to collect for years. In this crazy world, people are always cursing others, at least unconsciously, but this curse was heavy duty and placed "professionally."

Unfortunately, the healer became so immersed in negativity that he burnt out and quit, and died a few years later—it's not an easy thing to handle well, requiring constant clearing of one's matching pictures and maintaining a transpersonal stance.

10 EARTHBOUND SOULS

Earthbound souls are people who died but didn't properly transition to the astral plane. Instead, they are stuck on the etheric upper physical plane. Ghosts, who are attached to a particular building, are one kind.

Bars or places frequented by addicts can be full of earthbound souls who were alcoholics or addicts when they died and want to attach themselves to living people so they can continue to satisfy their psychological cravings. Addiction of all kinds tends to ravage a person's field, making it easier for negative energies to get in. (Healing the field, returning it to soundness, can help people release addictions.) In addition, people who previously weren't alcoholics, addicts, gluttons, or the like can suddenly become one due to possession by an earthbound soul via substantial holes in their aura. Successful "spirit releasement," as it is known in shamanistic work, can result in an instant cessation of these symptoms.

Hospitals are another problem area: people who have recently died but don't want to move on often hang out there, and patients undergoing surgery or other invasive treatments are especially vulnerable to possession. People who are ill don't have their natural psychic defenses, and surgery cuts open not only the physical body but the energy body as well. Many big problems often have their genesis during or shortly following hospitalization, and not for the obvious reasons.

There are degrees of possession, from partial (when we don't feel entirely ourselves) to more rarely, total, which can be confused with dissociative identity disorder. *The Unquiet Dead: A Psychologist Treats Spirit Possession* by Edith Fiore is a good book on the subject.

In working with earthbound souls, we may need to play psychotherapist, explaining to them that they've been stuck in a bad place and that we want to help them move on so they can be happier. It can help to find out why they've been hanging on and compassionately show them a better way. We then can call to their guides to accompany them to the light, and encourage them to go. To my surprise, I've sometimes found that earthbound souls are more likely to listen to an incarnate human being like me than to their guides. For one thing, some of them don't realize that they're dead and don't believe in spirits!

11 SOUL RETRIEVAL

The opposite of spirit releasement is "soul retrieval." Many judged, denied, or otherwise unintegrated fragments of ourselves can be lost in other people's energy fields or in the ether. (You'll probably encounter some belonging to other people in your clearing work.) Soul retrieval is calling these home. After releasing what isn't ours from our field, it's good to welcome back all parts of ourselves. For a more elaborate soul retrieval, you can work with a shamanistic practitioner.

CONCLUSION

I hope that this book inspires you to explore your field with curiosity about what's there, and gives you tools that lead to greater joy and freedom. Mastering energy is not so different from mastering a musical instrument—it takes daily practice, but we do get better over time, and the results are well worth it.

RESOURCES

Susannah Redelfs:
https://councilofone.org/techniques/

John Friedlander:
http://psychicpsychology.org/

Pat Kendall and Journeywork:
www.lifepathconsulting.com

Emotional Freedom Technique (EFT):
https://www.eftuniverse.com

My site:
https://shepherdhoodwin.com

ABOUT THE AUTHOR

SHEPHERD HOODWIN has been channeling since 1986. He also does intuitive readings, mediumship, past-life regression, healing, counseling, and channeling coaching (teaching others to channel). He has conducted workshops on the Michael teachings throughout the United States and Europe.

Shepherd is a graduate of the University of Oregon. He lives in Laguna Niguel, California.

ENERGY LITERACY

https://shepherdhoodwin.com

TWITTER:
@shepherdh
@EnlightenNitwit

FACEBOOK:
https://www.facebook.com/shepherd.hoodwin
https://www.facebook.com/shepherd.hoodwin.author/
https://www.facebook.com/JourneyOfYourSoul/
https://www.facebook.com/EnlightenmentforNitwits/

shepherdhoodwin@gmail.com

Summerjoy Press
99 Pearl
Laguna Niguel CA 92677-4818

OTHER BOOKS BY SHEPHERD HOODWIN

Available at https://shepherdhoodwin.com/book/

All Is Choice

Few realize how profound, multi-faceted, and far-reaching the concept of choice is in our spiritual growth. This short book explores topics such as what is and is not our right to choose, our power as creators and the limits of our reality creation, how consciousness expands, and much more.

Being in the World

This insightful book explores practical spirituality. Topics include aging, karma, time, and religion.

Compassion for Evil
A Metaphysical View

In this book, Shepherd explores the issue of evil from the soul's point of view, drawing on the channeled Michael teachings. Topics include karma, how souls evolve, the roots of evil, anger and fear, revenge, shadows, forgiveness, conscience, guilt, redemption, and love.

Embracing What Is
Spiritual Keys to Happiness

This book is an abridged version of *Happiness and the Michael Teachings*, without technical Michael teachings terminology. A free version is available at Smashwords.com.

Enlightenment for Nitwits
The Complete Guide

This hilarious metaphysical/self-help humor collection will appeal to Oprah and Dave Barry fans as well as those with more esoteric interests. In a style reminiscent of comedian Steven Wright, it's full of wry one-liners along with longer, hilariously mind-bending pieces on a wide range of subjects, tied together by the idea of clueless humans trying to find enlightenment.

"I love *Enlightenment for Nitwits*! It is the funniest book I have read in several decades. If laughter leads to enlightenment, it will certainly do it. Nothing—thank God—is sacred in this delightful spoof on life in general."
—C. Norman Shealy, M.D., author of *Life Beyond 100*

Growing Through Joy

This thought-provoking book explores the nature of

Happiness and the Michael Teachings
Learning to Embrace What Is

Happiness is the ultimate goal of every spiritual teaching. Here we explore several principles of what the Michael teachings refer to as growing through joy.

Healing the Gut
A Crib Sheet for Eliminating SIBO

This short ebook offers tips for those with digestive problems and related diseases, focusing on the Specific Carbohydrate Diet.

Journey of Your Soul
A Channel Explores the Michael Teachings

This is the most in-depth discussion of the Michael teachings to date. It may also be the first analytical study of channeling written by a channel. It has forewords by John Friedlander, author of *Psychic Psychology*, and Jon Klimo, author of *Channeling: Investigations on Receiving Information from Paranormal Sources*. Klimo writes, "*Journey of Your Soul* may well be the best (Michael) book of them all due to its clarity, thoroughness, and detail, and thanks to the fact that the author, an exceptionally clear-headed Michael channel himself, brings real integrity and authenticity to our understanding of Michael in particular and to the channeling process in general."

Loving from Your Soul
Creating Powerful Relationships

This inspiring, transformative book explores the nature of love itself as well as practical matters of relationships. One reader wrote, "There are phrases that are so inspiring that I wrote them down to refer to when I need them. I am looking forward to reading this book again and again."

Meditations for Self-Discovery
Guided Journeys for Communicating with Your Inner Self

This is a beautiful collection of forty-five vivid, often pastoral, guided imagery meditations channeled from Shepherd's essence. There are many meditation recordings available, but this is one of the first collections of meditations in book form that can be read to oneself or others. Teachers and group leaders would find it particularly useful.

Opening to Healing

This uplifting book explores the spiritual aspect of healing.

OTHER BOOKS BY SHEPHERD HOODWIN

Unconditional Love in Politics
Or Have You Hugged a Republican/Democrat Today?

Is unconditional love in politics an oxymoron? Thus far, it's been a rare commodity if it's ever been there. This book explores what you can do about it, as well as why both right and left have useful parts to play in our evolution, the factors that influence a person's tilt to the right or left, and what unconditional love might look like in this sphere.

Why We're Attracted
Spiritual, Psychological and Physical Elements That Draw Us to Others

Just why are we attracted to some people and not to others? This book explores a multitude of factors on three levels: spiritual, psychological, and physical. Topics include agreements, life path, soul chemistry, male/female energy ratio, celibacy, body-type attraction, sexual orientation, monogamy, and polyfidelity.

REVIEWS

Want to keep your practice fresh? Look here! Refreshing in its practical simplicity. A joyfully short book of practices that bring some great ah-ha moments relatively effortlessly!

This little blue book is helping me feel the underlying truth of my path, of my journaling practice and meditation, and the freedom in honest exchange. Many gems here.

Amazing. So inspiring.

Very helpful. Simply and well explained.

Printed in Great Britain
by Amazon